The Anchor's Long Chain

THE
SEAGULL
LIBRARY OF
FRENCH
LITERATURE

WORKS OF YVES BONNEFOY
AVAILABLE FROM SEAGULL BOOKS

The Arrière-pays
Translated by Stephen Romer

The Present Hour
Translated by Beverley Bie Brahic

The Digamma
Translated by Hoyt Rogers

Rue Traversière
Translated by Beverley Bie Brahic

Toegther Still
Translated by Hoyt Rogers

Ursa Major
Translated by Beverley Bie Brahic

Poetry and Photography
Translated by Chris Turner

Rome, 1630: The Horizon of the Early Baroque
Followed by Five Essays on Seventeenth-Century Art
Translated and edited with an afterword by Hoyt Rogers

The Red Scarf
Translated by Stephen Romer

The Anchor's Long Chain
YVES BONNEFOY

CENTENARY EDITION

Translated by
BEVERLEY BIE BRAHIC

LONDON NEW YORK CALCUTTA

PAP TAGORE
www.bibliofrance.in

The work is published with the support of the
Publication Assistance Programmes of the Institut français

Seagull Books, 2023

First published in French as *La longue chaîne de l'ancre* by Yves Bonnefoy
© Mercure de France, 2008

First published in English translation by Seagull Books, 2015

English translation © Beverley Bie Brahic, 2015

ISBN 978 1 8030 9 293 5

British Library Cataloguing-in-Publication Data
A catalogue record for this book is available from the British Library

Typeset by Seagull Books, Calcutta, India
Printed and bound by WordsWorth India, New Delhi, India

CONTENTS

TRANSLATOR'S ACKNOWLEDGEMENTS

I am grateful to the editors of the following publications where some of these translations first appeared: *PN Review* ('The Anchor's Long Chain', 'Tomb of Charles Baudelaire', 'The Mocking of Ceres', 'The Invention of the Flute of Seven Pipes', 'The Tomb of Giacomo Leopardi', 'Mahler, the Song of the Earth', 'To the Author of "The Night"', 'San Giorgio Maggiore', 'On Three Paintings by Poussin', 'Ulysses Sails Past Ithaca', 'A Poet', 'A Stone', 'The Tomb of Paul Verlaine'); *Notre Dame Review* ('The Tomb of Giacomo Leopardi', 'On Three Paintings By Poussin').

Beverley Bie Brahic

THE DISORDER

On the stage fifteen or so men and women stand close together, some of them facing towards the centre of the slowly shifting group. Each of them in turn steps away from the group, speaks, if this is what speaking is, and melts back into the group, unless he or she lingers to hear the next speaker. The faces are indistinct; one might think them masked.

....

She put the three or four photographs
Back in the drawer
And told him, with a smile,
Forget about remembering.

Our words?
Oh—like a funnel of smoke,
And these charred scraps of paper, our life,
Still making sparks.

He moves away, but she runs,
Catches up with him.

Take this, she says, take this chest
I hold in my hands,
The open box whose colours ripple.
Oh, love me!

He takes the chest.
The reds and blues swirl round them.
Simpler, colour even than life.
Through colour form breaks.

. . . .

Oh, he shouts, I wanted a voice
To enter the universe!
On the wide beach he turns towards his friend.
He looks at her; night is falling,
They walk off, they no longer see their footsteps in
    the sand where a little water shines.

And she says, Yes,
You have given away our life
For the spiral of a column's shaft,
Our life, you have pitched by the fistful,
Our whole life, into this form,

Our own beauty, you've thrown
Into the abyss of forms dreamt pure!

She stops talking,
She looks at the sea or maybe nothing
But the great face that stands
In front of those who are nothing but grief.

She walks away.
He can hardly see her now.
I should have been some fool you would have loved
For her silences, she says.
Her tattered songs,
Her feet dancing to the window on rainy days,
And then she stops, laughing, she turns round.

. . . .

This panel,
In front of the sky, a rectangle
Divided by a straight line.

And above, it is black, nothing but black;
Below, emerald green, like the sea.

What an enigma, what nothingness, this day, this
   night,
As we enter, both of us, our first bedroom.

....

I went outside,
Snow barred the earth.
Here and there in puddles it was still night,
The road hobbled along, down with the crow.
And I was dreaming of huge flames,
In my dream I fomented another sky.
Everywhere I wanted to be the axe
That would cleave the mass of what is,
The axe we hear
Endlessly thudding down in the valley.

I went out, it was cold, I weep,
O my friend,
All I can give you are chapped lips.

One day
You stopped being the free soul in me.

And yet, know,
We can think differently,
Think as when things are seen in the light of a
    beach.
Let the three Graces come,
And Apollo and Marsyas the flute player.

To be part of the sparkling,
Like a line of reeds between earth and sky.
And over there, in the sand,
The bird that is going to die but moves still.

To be
Like a voice paused at the summit of the song,
Where others join in. A book
Whose pages are white.
Some would say: Here are hands that hold a book,
Others: Its pages are white.
Others: Today's beauty,
Nothing but waves crashing on to the beach.
Nothing but a fringe of froth.

The song
So far beyond us, so much higher

Than breathing, than remembering.
This song, the wounded bird
That the sand is already covering.
It twitches, it is filled with death.

. . . .

She stood before him worn out with regret,
    disappointed love, and pain.
Naked, for the storm had flared up in the ruins
    of another storm;
In this way the wind
Changes the sky's form.

And in her hands
God knows what revolver from the bottom of a
    drawer,
Ageless anger
That throws itself shouting on the end of
    everything.

She opens the door wide, she is crying
Because he didn't know
Or only at the last minute,

And then her eyes filled with tears, but he
    was leaving;
I weep
For all those who have wept,
For the dead who go on dying,
For everything, even for the light that is within me.

But if I die he will die, he the eternal,
I must not die.
If I break down in the light he will break down,
Our clouds, our colours will drift,
High in the sky the winds will displace them
    irresistibly,
I must not die.

Oh, I have so much sorrow
That I am pure and have no more name and I
    sing almost.
I am no longer, I fall,
My head comes apart from one end to the other
    of the sky.

I am so alone!
They are going to burn damp branches,

Roll my life in a sheet.
Preoccupied, they talk of me this grey day
The wind sweeps through and whirls round.

Was it me, intact like the rushing sky,
Who grabbed at
This incomprehensible thing, the revolver?
When I close my eyes the steel feels heavy.
What god held up my poor fingers?
But now I have my small girl's hands back.

God,
God of others,
Look in my long day,
Look in my fatigue no one comes to lift from me,

Look in this blood
I am splashed to death with.

Look in the palm of my left hand,
Look in my right hand,
Look in my fingers I play at opening and closing.

....

We are a photograph that is torn up
The moment we love on this earth
But kindled by the lightning flash of that tearing.
See, it is this snapshot of an end of summer evening
    at the beach,
Naked children run towards the sea.

And the newspapers!
We pulled out pages, crumpled them into balls,
    tight balls,
Shoved them under the logs that refused to burn.
Smoke, smoke our life.
Now fire runs through the image,
Flames take the mouth, the smile,
Take the hand that clutches the fabric to the naked
    shoulder,
Take the gaze that no longer hides desire.
Oh, memories: our Erebus,
A great shapeless sob is at the bottom of us.

Tell me, what did you see in this packet, tell
    me quick
Before life is done!
I don't know,

A child's face maybe,
Maybe a body in a position, no, that's not the word,
    from this angle, no,
Maybe God's face.
But a force weighed on me faster
    than the images could slip.
I've gone looking so many times!
But their number—there's no end to them.
To hell with memory!

Do you remember
Our first bedroom? Do you remember the sad
Flowered wallpaper? We wanted to strip it off
Only there was other paper underneath,
Layers of it,
And the last, on the grey plaster, newsprint
With words from the other century
That we rolled under our wet fingers. At last
We scraped the wall clean with pen knives.
You were laughing, so was I, night was falling.

....

She dreams
She is up on the ladder, she knocks at the
    closed door.
The engines roar.
From the plane's belly no one responds
And the world takes off.
She hangs there adrift between birth and death
In the calm sky,
The sky where just a few puffs of cloud
Melt into the blue, that is, God—no, the eternal.

But this is a bad dream, isn't it,
This plane, God?
She turns over, she turns towards the shadows,
The curtains, the alcove's flowered walls
Too close to her face. Don't you see
I'm coming from far away, I'm coming from the end
    of the big beach,
I have my little boy by the hand, I'm cold, I'm alone,
Days follow days.

There were times I imagined I was Hagar
    in the desert
But the angel

Wasn't hovering over me,
Blue and red,
Nor appearing from a bush with the jug of water
and the bread.
I kept walking, what choice did I have?
And now, what bliss! I arrive, the doors open.

Come, my child,
Put your small hand in my big one,
Let's run,
The shadows of those rocks won't catch us.

They run.
Walls of foam break over them.
Colour's body in night's hands.

. . . .

At first hesitant
Trickle of voice. She steps out of the group,
Comes forward, shy
At the front of the stage.
It's a big thing
When speech comes back after so many months
of silence.

After months when she couldn't get up,
Fingers stitching, unstitching
The shapeless scrap of cloth on her knees,
Maybe she forgot,
She hummed a little, is that the right word?

But then, late,
They are back in the bedroom,
Men and women are rushing round,
They are moving furniture,
You hear the thud of furniture being dragged.

. . . .

And him,
As upright in his death
As a stylite,
His soul furled round him like smoke.

He shouts. From far we hear his cries;
Up closer they are words, senseless.
Is this about some wrong done to him
Before his first memories?
He doesn't see us, doesn't hear us,

If we go away, he'll still be shouting
Naked, up on his silly column,
Soiled, arms flapping at the sky.

. . . .

Look,
First the white mask then the red mask
But in their exchange see my face.

Look,
I bend my many faces over your face,
Smiling, we contemplate you,
With all our big hands I lift you up,
Under you the earth grows small.

O our child,
Come into our country where the sky is red,
Where maize hangs to dry over doorways,
Where rivers glint and afternoons don't end;
Come, that tomorrow your days run over
The pitcher you will set down on the stone,
And the evidence of the water, heat,
Tufts of the horizon, vibrating, bleached

By heat will be so strong
That you will be dizzy: this is being born.

....

He says: I am going to die.
My life ebbs and flows.
As in a little wood I saw
Flooded one long ago morning. Water
Was spreading under the trees. Currents formed.
They say that when you die thought grows calm
And that by degrees sorrows,
Life's enigmas fade.
But I—all I can think of
Is a name I've forgotten,
A name, oh so ordinary,
And time goes by and I throw away my last chances.

And yet all this sky through the trees,
These two twisted columns, the wisps of cloud
And that fire beyond the porch, where the archers
Shoot more and more arrows at us!

....

Children, sometimes, at night
When the lighthouse light starts to flash.
It's the top of a dune, they tumble down the slope.
What a lot of old stuff
Half-buried in the sand!
Coal, broken twigs, rags in many colours.
One of them, suddenly appearing up there
Waves a magazine page attached to a rod of
    some sort.
They shout. One boy falls onto one of the girls,
Wrestles. She thrusts her hand into the sand
    she grabs what sticks up, she tugs,
They both tug.
Newspaper, a sheet that doesn't end; torn,
    crumpled words.

. . . .

We are leaving each other.
Therefore we must remember,
But remembering is forgetting,
I will have forgotten you when I think I see
    your face.

Oh, please, she says,
Try to remember what doesn't destroy me.

Try to remember
This flower I am picking.

I want to suffocate between two colours, he cries;
I want to be in the dark and pitch handfuls of it
    at you,
I burn to die for you since dying is all I know.

And she:
What must I do so you can love me without dying?

No response, he just weeps.
The wind grows chilly, she reaches for her shawl.

....

Who would have thought, back then,
My friend,
The shepherd pushing his animals under the sky,
Washing the trembling ewe's
Swollen teat at nightfall,
That we would ever be ashamed of words?

That in naming the things which are
We might feel guilty?

That even saying, look,
Child,
We might feel guilty.

And it is true that snow falls over the snow,
That lightning prowls among our shadows in
     the whiteness of the snow.

That everywhere people shout, and they kill,

But, my friend,
Let us try to enjoy naming this morning again.
Let us go
Into these woods, boughs crusted with snow,

And look, there's a trickle of water in the creek,
And yet just yesterday you saw it
Utterly still, a prisoner of the cold.

THE ANCHOR'S LONG CHAIN
(ALES STENAR)[1]

I

They say
Boats appear in the sky
And from some of them
The anchor's long chain may rattle down,
Down towards our furtive land.
The anchor bobs over our fields and trees
Seeking a place to moor,
But soon a wish from above yanks it free;
The ship of elsewhere has no use for here,
Its horizon lies in another dream.

It may however come to pass
That the anchor is heavy, unusually so,
And rakes the ground, rumpling the trees.
Someone saw it snag a church door,

1 Ale's Stones, or Ales Stenar—59 boulders arranged in the shape of a
ship—is a megalithic monument in Skåne in southern Sweden.

Catch the arch where our hope fades,
And a sailor shinned down
The taut, jerking chain,
And freed his heaven from our night.
Such anguish as he toiled against the vault
Both hands grappling with his strange iron—
Why must
Something within us lure our minds
In this crossing our words attempt
All unknowing, towards the other shore?

II

What did he want, this country's prince,
To bring all these stones to the cliff,
So many stones upright in the shape
Of a ship that would one day
Sail off over the sea between sky and world,
And, ever hesitant, bewildered almost,
Maybe at last reach the harbour
Some seek in death, an imagined
Life more intense, a line of lights
On the deserted horizon of a long coast?
The nave of his desire,
This prow in the rock, these curved flanks,

Sails still. And I am trying to read
Into this stillness the movement he gave
To his dream, this captain
Who knew he'd die fighting masked men
Crying out in another of the languages
Of this world in which nothing endures
Save astonishment and pain.

One of the strangers from across the sea,
An envoy all in white light
In the smoke, beckons to him;
The prince fights back, he grunts, he shouts.
But already, with the angel smiling at him,
He falls silent, he withdraws to a cabin
At the bow of the ship, and they sit
Side by side, companions at a table
Where none of the charts,[2] the portolans
Of this life remain, none of the foods,
Nor even the images his memory
So readily offered him, at nightfall
In the strange country of birth and of death.

2 *Cartes*, meaning maps or charts (Yves Bonnefoy, email, 4 April 2014).

Memories of hours without battles,
Memories of words repressed,
Memories of the sweetness that is obscure
As the wine gravid in the grapes,
Memories of things seen, but not understood,
And too-brief moments of clumsy affection.

He dreamt, he departed. But today, here,
There is nothing before or around us
But the sky of this world, rays, wisps
Of cloud, then, on the darkened stone,
Thunder's arrow and the sudden rain.
A whole vehement water drenches us,
The steles now just a single presence
Here or there emerging, fading, though
Lightning plays in them. I want to believe
This flame means peace, a peace that embraces
With infinite emotion, infinite joy,
One who in this disorder fights—left, right—
Too many assailants, and is going to die.

Later, turning back
Towards the stone ship, under the sky
Bright now as a summer morning

(And what else to do but turn back
When nothing is that does not pass?),
I notice a large sea bird
Perched on the stone prow: an instant
Of mysterious stillness that lives
Without language are capable of.
The bird looks out to sea, listens, hopes,
It guides the ship, and others, others,
Are there round it, wheeling above it,
Mewling and turning into the wake.

AMERICA

I

Back then I was living in a cottage off by itself with a few others on a hill of sand and very bright, short grass. Early each morning I would walk down to a restaurant I could see a kilometre or two off, just on the other side of the road that follows the Pacific Coast, a little ways back from it. For me it was a pleasure to see the cars in the distance silently passing one another on this long ribbon of road on the edge of the deserted countryside; see, too, the windows of the restaurant whose night lights still gleamed, though day was breaking with its lovely golden light. Shadows—a car pulling up, one or two people moving towards a door—drifted past the panes. I descended a gently sloping road towards a life that seemed part of another world, although at some point the noise grew perceptible, then gradually increased; and the events of these peaceful minutes were never more than the sudden star of a fender striking a sunbeam or, on the long, low, blue mountain to my right, a mustard field's brief blaze. The daily life of the light, in short, a surprise intimacy but which from the start meant well, and reassured. The light was my friend, all day long it would go with me.

But on that day, a Sunday, what a change after all those mornings during which time flowed soundlessly like the ripples water leaves on beaches when the tide withdraws. Not a car on this road I could follow for kilometres from where I stood. In place of the usual weekday traffic I could see groups of what appeared to be children, all streaming in the same direction, rising from the northern horizon to descend under the southern one, and seeming even less a part of ordinary reality insofar as their entire time on this earth was spent, fantastically, clutching huge, often vividly coloured and even more astonishingly shaped balloons that bobbed in the air, up and down at different heights. Some of them very pure, the five basic forms, a perfect beauty of planes and ridges in the service of a translucent material, probably fabric; others complex, tangled, even at times vaguely clownish with their pointless extensions, arms and legs wearing bracelets or shoes of light. The balloons were on strings, which gave them a semblance of freedom, taken in good humour. And if some of these frail aerostats bobbed simply, vertically, along behind the small being in charge of them, others lurched and wobbled, chuckling, clumsy, debonair dragons, and yet others seemed to wander from one end of the procession to the other, on both sides of the road. Silky strings glistened, the garnet red, violet-blue or yellow of the fabric bellied like sails here and there turned opaque, now and then collided.

At times on the ground a stretch of bare pavement, but the procession—in which children might halt, turn round, backtrack, change groups—closed up fast, compact as before. Approaching the highway I could see that the crowd was huge, and here and there in its midst a variety of slender enigmas that I wouldn't, a moment before, have suspected. Sometimes what moved wasn't pedestrians but cyclists, one hand anchoring the string of a balloon that might be a pretty good size, some sort of fire-breathing montgolfier; some of the boys and girls were pushing or pulling wagons from which sorts of statues bobbed and swayed, flames on their shoulders too, or at least clouds of smoke, a rust-coloured vapour with incense I now could smell. The line went on and on, full of surprises. Just as powerful as the impression of the utter strangeness of this long parade, all but soundless as far as I was concerned, was its delightful endlessness. The grasshoppers that descend on the gardens of the last city before the desert are, I imagine, similarly mysterious: small lives, eyes shut beneath their tiaras of kings without kingdoms. But even more than astonishment what I felt was an overwhelming gladness, glad of marvels beyond understanding: the joy of hoping that yesterday's, forever's, chains of understanding will snap and that, in a state of unknowing, one will at last manage *to be* more.

II

Half-marvelling, half-musing, I was at the road. I went from grass to asphalt underfoot and began—just yesterday the cars had calmly braked to let me cross—to fray a passage towards my breakfast through clusters of children who, hooting, laughing, exclaiming, calling from swarm to swarm, ignored me. And I entered the restaurant where, like grasshoppers fallen from their cloud, several of the youngsters in the usual faded blue jeans, T-shirts or shorts, had also paused for red, white or in some cases yellow drinks. They were close to me now, some alone with their orange- or lemonade; I might have tried to discover the cause of this desert exodus but I kept to myself. It was enough not to imagine any sinister flute player marching them across the dunes.

I didn't question, I made no attempt to find out—someone within me whispered there was no point, it could only be an excuse for chitchat, small errors to note with amusement and promptly forget, for in fact I already knew, better than these laughing children, who, thank heaven, only wished to laugh and mill about, what was at stake in this long procession. A very big balloon, surely much bigger than most if not all the others, drifted, bobbing and shining, past the restaurant windows; a red glow lingered; easy to imagine it bobbing off somewhere further south, well after its thousands of tinier bounds, and landing in a place that could only be far away on the continent or out at sea—chance was the god of the day is what I had already sensed this gathering, this festival, meant. I was beginning to understand other things too; I saw this civilization's meaning clarifying for me, this America that I'd grown so accustomed to in recent years, even if it remained a little strange; as a matter of fact I deciphered all the mysteries, I even managed to elucidate a few of the events in my own life that I had struggled with in astonishment and distress. It was as if what showed itself to me on this California road was not just an event but a sign whose effect would be to deploy my thoughts henceforth in the image of these polyhedrons drifting by with their light-coloured surfaces—facets of life itself.—A whole intuition, a whole orderly series of ideas that I began to jot down, first on a corner of the table, then on a hillock or boulder on my trek back to my hillside cottage.

My jottings were mere phrases, highly elliptical, a word or two jotted on creased paper in the palm of my hand. Never mind. I would have time later—and tomorrow, and in years to come—to give a more explicit and finished shape to the explanation of America, and of everything that I had caught still flashing in my net.

III

That afternoon I had other things on my mind; then I returned to Paris. Weeks, months, years passed without me going back to my notes, until one day I said it was time to write 'America'. So I dug out the two or three sheets of yellow paper, torn from one of those American legal pads, my pencil marks already fading from between the pale lines: the paper had been folded and unfolded, in and out of pockets, abandoned on messy desks. I smoothed out my notes, I reread them, or tried to, for, at first glance, then second, then more—the examination increasingly perplexed and frustrating—I could make no sense of them. Words whose meaning had withdrawn. Of the greater coherence they had perceived and made note of, nothing, not even the hint of an outline. Some grey pencil marks among the paper's creases I finally decided were just lines, traced without reason within—not beyond—language's bounds.

I questioned myself. Hadn't I thought to make notes of the ideas I had that morning in California? Had I been foolishly trusting to memory; had meaningful thoughts which would now be valuable really and truly evaporated from the scrawled pages, leaving me deprived, maybe for all time, of my most essential truth? Or was I dreaming at the very moment I was writing, or so I thought? That long column of children, fantastic as it apparently was, had really happened in what one calls waking reality, I saw it much too clearly—I still see it now—but after? After, in the mind that interprets the signs? After, in the memories, the phantasms—and the feelings of illumination but right away the censoring —that the unexpected so violently awakens? My three pages of notes resembled nothing so much as those upside down formless and contentless words one so depressingly discovers on the paper one scribbled on in the middle of the night, in the wake of a big dream.

I asked myself these questions. Someone in me wished to reflect upon and to understand if not America and being in the world, at least the games my thoughts and my life play. But the perplexity, the desire were momentary; quickly the paper I was staring at darkened, words that refused to make sense began to swirl about, glow a little, and again there were images, blurred at first but soon quite precise as if I already knew much of what called out to me.

What was this dream? Well, still a procession, but this one on a narrow mountain path. Still schoolchildren, and their

balloons, but on a black windswept night. The children—
yes, definitely children, even younger ones than on the other
road—scramble unhesitatingly up nearly vertical slopes
where the path is so narrow between two rocks, one canti-
levered over the chasm, that they have to push and shove
across the dizzy threshold, on into the night. On they go,
eyes on the ground. Above them the almost invisible mass of
balloons tugging at strings that sometimes snap in the wind,
blowing blindly, foreign to the world. Sometimes I am shoved
aside by their numberless advance; at others I am swept along
with them, I share their stumbling, their fatigue, notice how
they pant, hear quick laughter here or there in the crowd, a
sudden few bars of song interrupted by cries of suffering,
tears. Sounds in space of balloons bumping, cracking, tearing,
striking the sky's waves of black air. Furtive flames alongside,
patches of red or yellow flare out. Sometimes the rumble of
falling rocks much higher up on the mountain, but all that,
all that always, silence. The biggest balloon has just drifted
by, only its underside visible, swathed in flame but not yet
burning. Later I will see it again; it seems to hover over a land
we don't see, that we will never perhaps reach, among the
stones, now under the whole sky, all the stars. And here
comes a child trying to make his way back despite the path's
narrowness—towards what? He bumps into the others, so

busy struggling forward and hanging on to their balloons that they don't even see him. I grab him by the arm, I stop him. 'Where are you going?' I say. His two eyes big with some idea I'll never know rise to meet mine.

And I ask him again: 'What is your name?' Without answering, pensive eyes still looking at me, he shakes his head.

I never forget you, child who wants to go back you know not where. Behind the least of these words I write I see you even when in their dreams my sentences have bright, if not very clear spheres at the ends of their breeze-tugged strings—spheres I could believe sparkle with dew as though day had returned to earth. I know you are in on the secret of all the paintings I love. I hear you stumbling in the stony depths of the few books I read, that I know how to read, your feverish face I want to take in my hands. Sometimes I almost touch your forehead, your questioning gaze, but then all these signs fade. And with them the day and the night, and even the world, even the wind.

CHILD'S PLAY

Child's Play

He was out walking in the woods when he heard the laughter, the shouts, the joy. What to do but stop, heart pounding, and listen to the children's voices through the scrim of branches, then chance going towards them, the other world? Pushing aside the branches and leaves that flicked gently at his face, he walked towards them. Acteon too pushed branches aside when it was nothing like faint laughter, rather a chasm that urged him on, from which smoke, acrid smoke, arose as if a fire had ignited some brushwood, soon to put an end to the world.

In a clearing a stage was set up. Very rudimentary, posts supporting a half-dozen lopsided boards, and three or four poles, odd lengths, to which a washed-out, holey rag was tied, fluttering between stage and sky. Behind, more trees, tall trunks, close together, soon dark. The stage occupied scarcely a metre of ground. The children scrambled up and down; a little girl, feet joined, had just jumped off but tripped; she'd fallen practically on top of a little boy in a red vest. Laughing. The boy rolls over, he pretend-pummels her, she cries, she pretend-cries.

He gives her a leg up, and with a flip she's on stage again, she turns to the audience, if there is one. 'I am the queen,' she proclaims, 'you are the king.' Indeed they are the queen and the king, the revelation has taken place, the test is over, night can fall this morning, the fire cease coiling its road of death under the dead leaves, the stones.

The Long Name

The sounds were monotonous in the extreme—each syllable linked to the one before without the slightest interruption, only now and again a slight swelling of the sonorous material as if to mark an emotion; and one understood that the woman's voice over there was calling. Over there? It was far away, surely very far away behind the curtain of trees that closed the garden on the sky side.

And he, who was walking towards the garden, had also, from very far away, heard, listened, and sped up to hear better, to reach the place the voice was coming from, or at least to get through the gates before it stopped. But it went on, the same—endless, was it—as what it had from the beginning no doubt been: diphthongs in which the *a* and *i* sounds predominated, in which the other vowels occasionally appeared and even, quite rarely, what could have been a sort of *e*, a mute *e*, and then the hint of a syncope. A brief instant of fatigue, disquiet? But no, the great voice promptly picked itself up and went on.

He found the gates open, he entered, he walked up the broad tree-lined avenue—with lassitude now for he was only a child and he had been walking for, I think I would have to say hours—and the park suddenly was all around him, countless lanes, quick bursts of bright colour in the sun angling down, and in the shadows smells that rose to meet him, long watery reflections behind the trees. Which way to go, he wondered, but already, leaving the avenue whose sand squeaked underfoot, he struck off between two bushes growing out of some thick tall grass. In front, behind, the voice continued telling its sounds, now high up in space, now skimming the ground. It was clearly very far away, but it could also seem to be right beside him.

He listens, making his way through the brush which can be brambles, his foot testing the stones beneath the grass, stones that sometimes crumble, roll, throw him off balance. He listens, he pictures this woman standing on a terrace, he sees her dressed in a red dress, behind her columns, massive carved doors, and in front of her a wide closed horizon of leaves, here and there pierced by flights of birds, wisps of smoke.

He listens—but right beside him he hears a completely different sound, that of a branch breaking close to the ground, and now, three steps away, a little girl his own age appears. She's wearing a white dress flared towards her feet whose little boots he glimpses, blue, stained with the green of trampled grass. Her hair is mussed, probably because of the brushwood that shoots out in all directions. She has seen him, she looks at him, astonished, unless she's lost in thought. Then she sits down on a stone. Behind her the sun outdoes itself, myriad spots of shadow move in the leaves that move, since now there's a bit of breeze that makes the park's myriad smells even more pressing. How many corollas in this fragrance, how many frail clusters whose colours also seem to be seeping out! And all this like a voice still, but a whisper, for that other voice over there goes on climbing high and clear into the light above the trees.

The little boy looks at the little girl. And she, while she arranges a small basket, a napkin-covered dish, a flask, some goblets, at her side, continues silently, almost sternly, looking at him. He too sits down, no, kneels, two steps back from her.

'What's that?' he asks.

'What's what?'

'The voice over there, and everything it is saying?'

The little girl studies him. A small wrinkle of amazement creases her forehead. Is she about to burst out laughing or is she sad? Hard to tell.

'The voice isn't saying anything. It's calling me.'

'Calling you?'

Yes, that's my name. And she—the woman—is my servant, who used to be my nurse. I am the king's daughter. And this morning I left, I don't know why, my father's palace garden. The garden is over there, through those tall trees. Maybe this is the garden too but between there and here is a very long fence I've been forbidden to cross. But there's a hole in the fence, and I risked coming here, coming here with my snack. I've been walking for a long time.'

She sighed.

'And she is calling you? She is worried?'

'Well, naturally. And I am going to go back. But I still have time.'

She sighed again.

'Because she hasn't finished saying my name yet.'

And indeed the voice carried on tossing up into the darkening air syllables in which the *a* predominated but in which there were more and more *i* sounds, including sounds which were both empty and full, as when water hits stones. The voice flowed on undiminished, rather its banks spread out; one sensed that the call, in its confidence or its distress— how to know which—was taking as witness a whole horizon of blue mountains between whose summits frontons and domes emerged, beyond the very thick, very green wood.

'Your name!' the little boy says. 'That's your name?'

'Oh, I know it is very long,' the little girl murmured. 'When I was born the king my father found I was so beautiful!

Seventy-two times more than God,' he cried. And since the name of God has seventy-two syllables my name had to have seventy-two times seventy-two. Or so he thought for the first week.'

'Oh—and after?' the little boy exclaimed, sitting down now at the little princess' feet.

'After? The king my father estimated that I was seventy-two times more beautiful than he had thought the first day, and that my name had to . . . '

She starts to cry. Through her sobs:

'My name never ends,' she says. 'When my nurse comes to wake me up in the morning, it takes her so long to say my name that something always happens to cut her off. So I never hear my whole name, and I don't know what all I am, it is as if she'd never really wakened me, I can't shake off sleep, it is my dream that wakes up, taking me with it, at times for days. I wash my face in a dream. I drink my glass of milk in a dream, I go in a dream into the garden. Right now maybe I am in the middle of my dream.'

'I don't want you to be dreaming right now,' her friend replies, 'for then I would not exist and I would be sad.'

'Oh, me too,' the little princess exclaimed. 'What can we do so you really exist?'

'We can wait for her to finish, then you'll be awake, you can get up and come and walk with me on the other side of the fence.'

And he added, 'You will come to my house.'

She looked at him with interest. But the voice went on and on. The princess opened her basket, extracted two pieces of bread and butter, some salt in a paper cone, hard-boiled eggs, shelled. They ate that, and also some grapes, without talking. They drank from the flask, they put the goblets back in the basket. It was dark.

'Listen,' he says again, 'I have an idea. What if you changed your name? If you renamed yourself . . . ?' He thinks. 'If I called you . . . .' He doesn't dare speak aloud the name he has found, yet he murmurs it—two syllables as with his own name, the same syllable twice; she must have heard it. 'What do you think?'

The little girl shook her head, sighed, her eyes once more full of tears. But she smiled. And opened her mouth to respond. But all at once the voice behind the trees over there stopped. Such silence—never before in the world had there been such silence! Nature's silence. The silence of those great valleys one perceives without being in them, because only one's thoughts go towards them on mornings when one has been very far, to the edge of the cliffs. He, who had come so far, who had listened so intensely, he looked dumbly at his friend, his new friend. She seemed edged with a light phosphorescence. But her smile was fading.

'You can see they are calling me,' she says. 'It is time to go back.'

She stood, collected her basket and the flask, made the most graceful of curtseys to the little boy, turned round and vanished into the bushes that were black now because from everywhere night was falling over the world.

With his foot he gave the boat a shove and it bobbed away from the bank and drifted downstream, stranding him at the foot of these big rocks. And he, who had been rowing for a while, ever since he had embarked on this crossing the previous day, shook off a trace of light-headedness, then climbed the first escarpment, easily since there were sorts of steps, though narrow and uneven, between some of the stones. Sparse yet almost blue grass grew between the slabs. Wind had deposited sand, small reddish-ochre beaches that ants filed across. He watched one of them for a while, zigzagging he'd have said for nothing. Then he was at the top; he straightened and gazed at the horizon.

There before him, and to his left and to his right, was a plateau of thicker, taller grass now and then swept by shadows that glimmered like the puddles left by overnight rain undulating gently off into distances that seemed to rise from under the earth, long thin lines of blue hills whose tops shimmered in the dawn light. Dotted about this wide open space he could also see a number of trees, sometimes close together and even forming small thickets, elsewhere completely alone;

these didn't feel essential to the landscape, the prairies being so vast and the trees in the background, some of them perched on the rim of one of the hollows that modulated the plateau. They weren't the essential, they were not what the plateau's immensity offered to that of the sky. Still, some appeared very tall, with majestic crowns.

He takes a few steps now, although there are no paths in this grass of the end of the world—in this silence—and soon finds himself at the foot of an oak; he stops, he looks at it, he waits: because this majesty, this beauty asks him to wait, and even to sit down, which he does, on one of the stones that breaks, he now notices, through the grass's fabric, but without tearing it, or hardly. What to do, though, when one is seated at the base of a big tree? When one hears stirrings in the branches, maybe birds, or leaves a breath of air rustles? 'Count us, count us,' a blade of grass seems to say. He counts a little, but really he'd rather dig a hole in the ground with both hands, and free the brown earth, which seems cool, then stretch out in this grass and press his face into its cleft.

He stands, he walks on. In a landscape like this, one goes from tree to tree, even if they are, as is the case, farther apart than one might have thought. How long does he walk before he comes to the foot of this other oak? Whose stout gnarled roots have lifted the ground in all directions, pushing themselves towards him, who slows down, intimidated, who stops a second time. Above him the dais of tightly knit branches— it is dark here, even if it is still morning. Overhead a bird shakes the foliage, lumbers off, but he will not have seen it. Why? Could it be because of this little boy who pops up in front of him?

A child, indeed, in short trousers, feet bare, knees blotchy red. His forehead is low, hair tumbling down. Expression sulky, maybe sullen. Both fists held out, closed over who knows what; he comes up, very close, too close, he looks the new arrival—is this the right word?—in the eyes, insolently, flings open his hands. The closed thing is marbles. One drops, he snatches it up—not easy because the others could roll away. There, he has it; he unbends. 'Will you play with me?' he asks.

The one who is being asked hesitates, he really hesitates. Then he answers, 'No, I don't want to.'

'Well then, come on, let's run,' the little boy says, and he turns his back and takes off running with a shout, 'You can't catch me!' And the other child runs after him in all this green that whips his face, that blinds him. Where did my friend go, he wonders. Behind the oak? He walks round the oak, but there's nobody there on the prairie with no other trees nearby. He waits a moment. He starts walking again.

And an hour or two later it is noon in the sky. On his way he has seen trees, small woods but hasn't gone up to them, and now here he is under a big elm, unless this elm, which is huge, is an unknown kind of fruit tree—splotches of colour here and there in the grass do look a lot like fruit. The little boy walks under the elm, he has been in its shade which is cool, pleasant, for a moment; he'd like to stop and rest but he hears laughter. A light, high-perched laugh, maybe ironical. Who can be laughing so in this deserted place? It must be up above, up in the branches? He lifts his head.

And there she is, a small, bare-legged girl astride a branch. Her hair is every which way and her dress is some kind of red rag. Her hand is outstretched, index finger pointed straight ahead of her at who knows what, laughing. 'Who are you?' he exclaims. She looks at him. 'I don't know,' she says, 'I am playing.' Quickly she adds, 'I am playing at waiting.' A short silence, then the same light, slightly high-pitched laugh.

He doesn't laugh, he is sad. 'Who are you?' he asks again, and it is as if he were pleading.

But she won't answer any more, she has let her arm drop, closed her hand; she stares at her fingers, her wrist, thoughtful, and again that laugh, and a minute or two later, same thing. He walks away.

And his tread is more plodding now, and halting, for from time to time behind him in the tree he hears the little girl's laugh, and then he turns round, he sees the tall elm standing alone against the sky, then growing less distinct and even hard to make out when through an effect of distance other trees nearer or farther away interfere with its image. At one point he no longer recognizes it, and the laugh too gets effaced from the overall silence, if not from his heart.

By now it is very late in the afternoon and the colours are changing, the sun has dipped under the high-up blue that seemed endless; it is descending towards the hills of that other world over there, and wind is moving the grass, birds are singing—as for the person who keeps walking, walking, what makes him think that this is a road, what he has been following in the grass? Why does he believe that these are signs, what he sees drawn or painted on the stones, the first stones to show themselves so openly today? Grey stones. More and more of them, which finally rise and meet at the foot of an escarpment where a tree springs up, a big tree.

What a big tree! It climbs skywards like smoke. But it has thick blue branches like arms reaching out in all directions, to embrace one might say, without knowing whom, though, in this sky where there is nobody.

And when one gets close to it, like the child now, one sees that its leaves are broad, shiny, with coppery red veins ramifying into a green that doesn't exist anywhere in the mind. A green like an abyss, an abyss in which storms could be rumbling.

'I will stop at the foot of this tree,' the wanderer tells himself. 'I will kneel in its grass. I will pick its fruits, which are as big as the world. I will drink the water I know is bubbling up from under its roots. I'll climb its trunk . . . .' He feels exhilarated, he forgets his fatigue, but why doesn't he clamber up the rocks round the tree, the rocks where there are sorts of steps, even if they are narrow and uneven? Something in him resists, he has felt his fists clenched, one of his knees buckles, he walks faster, he flings himself onto the big meadow which, just there, grows steeper in front of the sky, a slope among yet more trees, yes, and at the end, where there are more trees, something resembling the edge of a big wood, or a forest, in the darkness in which nothing at all is any longer visible.

Evening advances, though the light stands still. The traveller in this land of prairie and pools of shadow goes his way; he walks past more oaks, more elms or some maples in larger and larger clumps with bushes at their feet now, almost woods and brush. The edge of the forest is close, he crosses it; soon he is under the leaves, he walks on without turning back in this forest where everything is path, where nothing goes anywhere.

Has she been dreaming, is she still dreaming, does she want to dream now? She tugs her little skirt down over her knees, she sticks out her bare legs, she sees her bare feet, touching at the little bump below the nail, on the left in the right foot, on the right in the left foot. She is five, six years old, something like that. She is sitting on the tiled floor, the door in front of her is open, it is summer, the weather is fine, outside the sky is big and calm.

If she jumped up, if then she were on the threshold, if she went out, she would see the grass, the big trees fairly evenly distributed across thick grass off into the distance over there, and nothing else. To left and right of the door, against the wall, just this road, that comes from behind the house, passes in front of it, disappears. A paved road, the same grass growing between its old disjointed stones as everywhere else on earth.

A road? What is a road, and why? Take it on the right, and disappear with it? What's the point of disappearing? The sky is so big and so still in the heat. The world is so much bigger when one looks at it through the outline of a door. She won't get up from the vestibule's tiles, coolness, lozenges of light and dark ochre.

And besides, this small music, at times. Like the minimal trails of white cloud she sees float past on the blue. Floating past, no. The minute they appear—on the left—they melt away, they never reach the part of the sky that is hidden on the right by the door.

All is peaceful.

Only the music grows louder, and now it is noise as well, tumult in its depths, a chaos of sounds, a din from below, they are coming, they are here!

Five, six musicians fill the door. A pushing shoving crowd of them, each thrusting his head between the other heads because he too wants to get a look at what is inside, inside where she is, wants to see her, she who sees them—and though the opening is wide it is way too small for so many instruments. The violinist has flung himself down on the ground, he slides his violin under the feet of the others, with his bow he works at the melodious little box that he has more or less managed to yank into the vestibule. How long his arms are, and how beautiful his melody, even though he keeps bursting out laughing, the dumbbell!

But the flautist has his leg over him, and his flute would be in the entry too, except that the oboe and the cymbals and the humble panpipes and the proud tuba need some room too, and the viola da gamba, and also the tambourine that the tambourine man must lift high up so it is visible, but it is true that his arms too—the tambourine man's—go on for ever.

And the harp, and the serpent! As for the harpsichord, it comes running, it is just a little late because it takes two to carry it, two of these boys, of these young women. How heavy it is, a harpsichord, when your feet sink into the ground, still full of puddles after last night's shower!

For sure the harpsichordist will have mud on his long legs. And now here is a bugle unless that's a hunting horn going by, its face hilarious in the middle of all this confusion which, this is the word, enchants its spectator. Look at her looking with her mouth agape!

And don't imagine that she can tell the panpipes from the harpsichord, but what good is knowing when one hasn't time for things to make sense? She is learning not to know.

And besides the musicians have already left, with their harmonies, their cacophony. It is even unlikely they ever came, the white clouds are too peaceful, the little bump on the left foot touches too eternally the little bump on the right.

The Painter Whose Name Is the Snow

What crimson over there, where the sky has toppled!

So the snow came in the night, bringing colour in its hands.

Silence is the name of all it bestows on us.

Adam and Eve go by on the road, muffled up. Their footsteps make no noise in the snow that covers the grass.

The mist pushes back thin curtains for them, makes a room among the trees, then there is another one, and another one.

A squirrel shakes itself, from too much light.

No one has been in these woods before, not even he who names and agonizes over having named and dies,

God who is no more than the snow.

II

This painter bent over his canvas—I touch his shoulder, he jumps, he twirls round, it is the snow.

His face is without end, his hands without number, he climbs, he goes to the left, he goes to the right of me and above me in these thousands of flakes that fall thicker and thicker, brighter and brighter. I look behind me, snow everywhere.

His brush—a wisp of smoke at the top of the trees, which melts, which melts him.

III

Sometimes all I can see is my shoe punching holes in the squeaky white. The laces' bright blue, the close-woven ochre canvas, the brown blotches left by the snow, that slides off as soon as my foot frees itself so as to carry me on into the swirls of light.

The painter called snow has done a good morning's work. He has spruced up the branches' outlines. The sky is a child that runs towards me laughing; I wrap the thick wool scarf more warmly about its neck.

God cannot want us to give him a name, so they thought, for the idea of a name suggests that of subject, verb, predicate: we will expect God to be this or that, we will look for him to do this or that in one of our perceptions, which will be in opposition to others, we will fight for one or the other—in his name we will tear one another apart. A name for the absolute is not a designation, even less a celebration—no, it is the trap language sets for us. The name of God is the problem. Name God and right away the wheat burns, the lamb's throat gets slashed.

But hardly had they come to this—banal—conclusion than their anguish flared up. For standing in front of a field of wheat, with the name of the wheat on the tips of their tongues, thinking of the beauty of the wheat, its presence, its absoluteness, they feared having already named God somewhat, and thus having erred. As they gazed at the wheat in the sun, the name one must not conceive of flitted past like a shadow, and now, quivering, there it was darkening the vineyards on the hillside and the water glittering in the stream. Everything they so legitimately loved was the occasion to commit an offense. All thought was risky, and all conversation, especially with those they loved, because one exalts what one loves, one finds what exists divine, one is eager to talk about it. Their walks in the evening light were a cause for fear; they hardly took any, or only with their eyes cast down; even worrying about these too-blue stones the Devil had perhaps had left on their path. The lovers' bed was dangerous. Teaching involved the use of constant, tiresome abstractions, since to allude to the rose, to the wine, in the beauty of a poem gave a glimpse of things that by participating in the being of God deprived the spirit of the good which is his absence in words.

Should they stop looking for fear of seeing? Touch nothing, or only with such instruments as keep things at a distance like the robotic metal arms used to penetrate fire, cold, the extremely small, or the void?

The upshot was that, more and more, they banished from their lives occasions they only too often had to love something or other in the world. They made their days and nights a void, indefinitely. Their words too. They renounced the representative arts, and even art that evokes and seemed great in aspiring only to evoke, with its excited and naive enthusiasms. Everything whose seriousness they could fear they renounced, for seriousness dotes on affections, values, memories. Unable to truly blind themselves, truly stop talking, they organized what might seem to be events, shows, but of the sort one only glances at in passing, without much interest, because one has so many other things to do. These took place on the shore, preferably at night. Men were unloading huge chests from a boat. They were piling them on the puddle-soaked quay. They were dragging them round, heavy as they appeared to be from the big iron bars rolling round inside their closed-up being. This is 'playing God', they said. Better to play God than to venerate him since one venerates with metaphors, and metaphors fragment, and the fragmented is death.

They resolved to die, because God—it was too much to go on living. Without further ado some committed suicide. Others were dragged down by a sullen indifference. And died too, when their time came. You can see their civilization's remains on this island. Even in ruins the temples are beautiful. Masterly statues still stand on their walls, often smiling, eyes leached of colour, long, supple hands. Some are naked men and women with tremendous innocence in their stance, but also something tremendously sad, as if they had a premonition of what was to come. Must we think—what a paradox—that this art was too beautiful, that it aroused excessive joy? It seems, in any case, that one day a being with a strange, bleak faith came along, someone who decided that humanity is guilty of having around and in itself objects worthy of love, and beings whose hands one can happily take in one's own: springs whose cool water we can drink. God is more, he cried. Not understanding that in setting fire to everything he still gave his god names, fire, death; and betrayed the one who, perhaps, needed us to invent happiness for him—a god who would have enjoyed sharing his name with everything and nothing on earth—being the wheat field, being the sun, being the hair spread out in the dusk of the bed, being, eternally, the wind's leaps, the tuft of grass.

II

We've come down from higher up towards the shore. The chapel is built right on the edge of the beach; it is, in fact, a simple *pisé* hut, its one small window bisected by an iron bar. Thick grass grows all around it, even in the doorway—we had to work to get it open. A palm tree spreads its precarious shade over the tile roof, patched with branches. Almost noon.

My guide, my friend, turns the old key in the old lock, and we enter. Within, nothing but a white sandy floor, a few wizened oranges, already almost blue, pushed into a corner, and facing us, set on the ground, as if abandoned, a statue or rather the roughed-out shape of one. The saint's head has not even been started; in the block of dark wood one can just about make out the form of the body which the sculptor seems to have intended to be standing, one leg in front of the other, torso naked above one of those long pieces of cloth water bearers or scribes wore in Egypt, an Egypt which, to be sure, is not far away—over there towards the south, a mere two or three days of uncertain navigation, with those different sands and oases whose smell is often perceived here on the island we're on, the big island facing the big river, the mountain-island that between nothing and nothing rises into the clouds.

The saint's head hasn't been started. Still, I take the chunk of wood in my hands, I lift it, it is quite heavy, I look at what is closer to completion in this work of a few days, but also perhaps a few centuries ago—the hands clasped over the chest, holding what appears to be a sphere, if a very rough one, the sculptor not having attempted to evoke the smoothness and fullness of a volume as geometry conceives it. I quickly see that this roughness was not feared, was even perhaps sought. It looks as if the fingers of the unknown being squeeze this thing—its matter seems to yield a little to their pressure.

I put the statue down, I look up, look round me in the room; nothing else catches my eye, unless it is the colour that flakes off alongside the roof beams where water seeps in when it rains, probably rarely. The door has swung shut, only a ray of sun but intense, blinding, filters between its dark wood and the wall. As for my guide, he has gone out; I think I hear him talking with some children.

I saw those children earlier. The biggest on his bicycle, zigzag-ging next to his friends, one foot scraping a beat-up shoe on the ground. And the two or three others so young that at least one goes naked, in the light. Their bodies are like the bronze of the statues Egypt will not have had, a bronze that seems burnished by the fires of a setting sun. I told myself in passing that they know. They know; or at least haven't yet totally forgotten.

PASSERBY, DO YOU WANT TO KNOW?

I

Passerby, do you want to know
How the guest of this tomb died,
This student bent over his books?

One night he was reading
Saint Augustine's treatise, the *De Trinitate,*
Before his grate in which a flame flickered.
Wind rocked the house
Standing in the middle of neglected gardens
And his rented room. From time to time
Waves of rain crashed over the windows;
At other times, silence.

What he was reading?
'God does not signify,
God alone.
God is the only reality that is only thing,'

(For every thing, you see,
The book explained,
Is sign, sign of another thing. Even stone,

Even the roughest lump of stone most absent
From the soul's councils is still sign,
Of chaos, let's say, of nothingness. Only God
Refers only to himself.
The very thought of sign is lost on him.)

And the student dozing over his book
Mused: what does it mean
To be merely that, a thing,
With nothing, with absolutely nothing
To allow us to grasp
The instinctive need to create meaning,
To name? Stone, immense stone,
I know how I love it, as perhaps
One may love God, but only
In giving it a name: this name, stone, its name,
And so taking it, as our eyes open,
Into our place of names, our refuge.
Thinking towards the outside—
We can't. Conceiving the without-name,
The without-capacity-to-signify—
We can't; this would be like stumbling
Over a body in a grave.
Because that which doesn't signify
Is death, it is death, death alone;

Death is what, under each word, escapes our grasp.
And if the sound at the base of a word
Torments us, now and again,
When a syllable trips us up,
If within us something, suddenly,
Stops speaking, doesn't signify, yawns like a pit,
We recoil from the brink
And, swaying, legs heavy, prickling,
We let ourselves fall
Into the world's thick grass that is us.

For if God is only thing
Why want him? Him—the outside,
Him—who would lay waste to all our memories?

II

The student reflects
Then—what was that noise? he shudders.
He stands, steps back from the hearth,
Turns off two or three of his weak lamps.
Little more than the thought now
Of the scattered coals, sometimes flames
That trace on the ground fire's words.
Yes, there's some sort of moon outside

As in literature, one of those moons
That like to give meaning to wind and rain,
But the sky is seething, and clouds
Keep covering it. And the person listening
To the night sounds perhaps remembers
Those of his childhood. He wasn't asleep,
No, he was listening
To trains from the world's far-off places
Shunt past down in the bottom of his suburb's gardens
With that noise that has reason to be
So does some good, and brings sleep.

He is thinking, he watches his table
Stretch, cast itself far into the shadows,
Shining, almost, and black. Suddenly
Against the pane, the tick of a pebble
Tossed by someone, that bounces off
The sill outside, then ceases to exist.

What was that? Wasn't it the same tap-tap
That distracted him from his reading earlier?
He holds his breath, he listens—
The garden is quiet, even the wind
Drops, the rain only flicks at the pane.
Should he be worried? The temptation

Is to forget, to efface
The sign in the noise, to trust
In the non-significance of the night.

Yes, but here's a pebble
Pinging the glass,
Then again, loud as before.

And this time
He's really afraid, now he does it—throws
Open the window. Ten steps
Off, a phosphorescence. A woman,
Old, in rags. Tall but stooped,
With her hands moving, one
Holding a fistful of pebbles still.
This woman, some grey, some yellow almost red,
All running together in what looks like
A painted figure, against some fissures,
And about it the rain is folded
Like a shawl, no, a mandorla.
He has seen her before, he knows
He has, has clasped the thin hands
In his hands, on a table. Sooty,
He remembers, black with the grime
Of the old hearths close to the ground

Over which kettles were hung;
Hands, yet, elsewhere in her eyes, a little girl.
Who are you, O wanderer? he asked.

Who are you? But now she has a ring
On her head, a ring that looks like iron,
Flames rise from. A whole tiara
Of damp sparks that quiver, flutter,
Almost sputter out. This scene
Seems to be happening far away—but how fragile
A fire that water covers, and this woman
Whose hands move the colours, how close she is!

He knows, seeing her, that she wants
To come in, to come up to his big table,
On it lay her hands, which will have laid
The crown, still burning, on the ground.
'Who are you?' No. 'Come in,' he says.

III

'Come in,' he repeats, and she smiles
Through the rain that makes her face glisten.
Come in! She walks towards him, she stumbles,
he catches her,
She crosses the threshold.

And around him the house fades,
And around her in the brightness
Of the flames on her head that push and shove
As if to push into another life.
She has come in, they stand in high grass,
Underfoot there are holes, and he is afraid
The bending flames will gutter out;
But nothing in the sky can do anything to them
Except multiply their colours
Ever new, in the mist
Of this night that weighs on them with all its weight.

They are going to fall down
Sooner or later, over there.
On their knees, they will look at each other.
Deeply furrowed, the woman's face.
'Who are you,' he will ask again, but, graciously
And even smiling
She will take the tiara from her head,
Set it down beside him in the grass.
Then she will stand and walk away,
Having paused a moment, nonetheless,
Immobile, then turned away,
Tilting her head towards her shoulder
The way little girls do
Whether from flirtatiousness or pain.

And he,
Bent over the tiara whose enigma
Shines through the leaves and stems
Of the tall water-blurred grass, he knows
That, were he to rub
One of these lights between his finger and thumb—
No, it wouldn't burn him,
And it would stay upright.

He knows that were he to try
To snuff out the flame, stubbornly
Attempt to douse it
With the mud under the grass, this flame
Would dart up triumphant.

The tiara,
Is nothing, he notices, nothing
But a theatrical prop—two rings
Close together yet separated
By four or five wire staples.
One of the circlets fits round the head,
The other holds the seven cups
In which some sort of oil doesn't stop bubbling.

ALMOST NINETEEN SONNETS

Tomb of L.-B. Alberti[3]

Did he dream this facade was his tomb?
He sensed the harp in the stone
And wished the sound of these arches
To be gold without substance, poetry.

Change nothing,
He would tell his assistant, or else death
Will play havoc with proportion, you'll destroy
'All this music', our life.

The facade incomplete, like any life.
But its numbers are children at their games
Of being the gold in the water they play in.

They jostle one another, they fight,
They shout, they splash one another with light,
At nightfall they run off, laughing.

3 A 'tomb' or *tombeau* is a composition, poem or piece of music, written in memory of a great artist; for example, Stéphane Mallarmé's 'Le Tombeau de Charles Baudelaire', or Maurice Ravel's 'Le Tombeau de Couperin'.

Tomb of Charles Baudelaire

Standing close to you, whom words fail
As evening comes to your astonishment
On this earth, I imagine only
The ones, to us unknown, of the woman

You called a pensive Electra,
Who sponged your burning brow,
And 'with a light hand' dispelled
Dread from your feverish sleep.

Mysteriously you pointed to her,
For being compassionate is itself
The mystery that makes these three letters,

J, G, F, loom large in the light
That guides your boat. Being for you
Harbour at last—its porticos, its palms.

'Facesti come quei che va di notte . . . '[4]

He was swinging a sort of torch
Whose double beam disconcerted
Those who came behind who tried
Not to be afraid, walking on the brink.

Guide, why doesn't your body shine
With any of this light you provide?
Do you not need to see the ground
Caving in underneath your feet?

Such is allegory's fate—he who speaks
Cannot and must not know the source
Of his words nor how deep their roots.

He seeks his footing even in the void.
In his words flight hesitates and swerves,
Flames less with dream than ashes.

4 Dante Alighieri, 'The Purgatorio', *The Divine Comedy*, Canto 22,
l. 67: 'You did as he who goes by night . . . '

The Mocking of Ceres

Out of friendship for his fever's words
He peered through the fogged-up pane
Of his sleep. People were talking outside;
He opened his door a crack, it was night.

Painter, whose hand is this you grasp
In your own hand when you're asleep?
Why cling to it, this child's hand,
As if its grip it might set you free

From a fear that ravages your images?
I dream you guide its trust
Right to the judge, she who condemns,

But loves, and suffers. Reconcile the child
With the desire. So that there be in him
No more astonishment, in her no vindictiveness.

The Tree on the Rue Descartes

Passerby,
Look at this tall tree, look through it,
It may suffice.

For even in tatters, soiled, a street tree,
It is all of nature, the whole sky,
Birds perch in it, in it wind moves, the sun
Speaks of the same hope, in spite of death.

Philosopher,
What luck to have the tree in your street,
Your thoughts will be less arduous, your eyes
Freer, your hands more desirous of less night.

The Invention of the Flute with Seven Pipes

At some point in the last of his tales
He began, in his fearful words, to run,
Seeing that a threat hung over him,
Looming larger with every word.

As if, from the colours that each thing's
Impenetrable name dissociates
Or, from the sky the wind's name
Opens, a wave broke over his life.

Poet, will music suffice to save you
From death with the help of this flute
Of seven pipes, that you invent?

Isn't that just your voice running out of breath
So your dream will last? Night, nothing but night,
Those reeds rustling under the bank.

Tomb of Giacomo Leopardi

In the Phoenix's nest how many have burnt
Their fingers stirring the ashes!
His consenting to so much night
Allowed him this harvest of light.

And his confident words held
Not some onyx up to a black sky
But their cupped palms for a drop
Of earthly water and your reflection,

O moon, his friend. He offers you some of this water
And, bending over, you want to drink
Of his desire, and of his hope.

I see you, coming close to him on these bare
Hills, his country. At times ahead,
Turning back to laugh; at others shadowing him.

Mahler, the Song of the Earth

She comes out, but night has not fallen,
Unless it's the moon that has filled the sky;
She goes, but also she is waning,
Nothing left of her face, nothing but her song.

Desire to be, know when to renounce;
The things of the world ask this of you,
How solid they are, each thing in itself
In this peace the dream shimmers through.

May she, who is leaving, and you, ageing,
Go on walking under the trees;
Sometimes you glimpse each other.

Oh speech of sounds, music of words,
Turn your steps now towards each other
As a sign of complicity, still, and regret.

Tomb of Stéphane Mallarmé

Let his sail be his tomb, since no
Earthly breath could persuade the skiff
Of his voice to refuse
The river, summoning him to its light.

Hugo's most beautiful line, he would say:
'The sun set this evening in the clouds';
Add nothing, subtract nothing from water—
It turns to fire, and to that fire he is yoked.

We see him over there, a blur at the prow
As his boat fades from sight, waving
Something our eyes here can't make out.

Is this how one dies? Who is he speaking to?
And what will be left of him once night falls?
That dent in the river, his two-coloured scarf.

To the Author of 'The Night'[5]

He entered his tomb before he was dead—
His usual evening city, absent the crowds.
The big door black. In the distance still
A few passersby. Then no one in the night.

He went down one street, then others, others.
A cart, once. The driver eyeless
And faceless too. And then again
Nothing but his footsteps' echo.

Gates he rattled at locked courtyards,
Doorbells, doorbells, whose ringing
Died out in stairwells of empty houses.

He groped down stairs, towards a quay
Where the river still trickled.
Listened to the sound of time running down.

5 Guy de Maupassant, 'The Night: A Nightmare' (1887).

San Giorgio Maggiore

Can it be that behind these walls
Noble as the child who came naked
Lies only a suite of ill-lit rooms, one
Opening on the next, ad infinitum?

Such is the Intelligible's misfortune—
Its dream takes the form in its hands,
Such fibrillations in this light!
Absence's artery is throbbing.

And hands meet, here is the porch,
But to wield the blade of a sacrifice.
At symmetry's peak the lamb dies.

Architect, liberate from this blood
The hope of which the stone's form speaks,
That is the price of the light's good.

On Three Paintings by Poussin

His tomb, you ask? But it's this space
He left hollow, dark under the leaves
Of the tree where old Apollo meditates
On what's young, and so more than god.

It is also this chink of light
In the *Birth of Bacchus,* when the sun
Takes hope, not yet tarnished, in his hands
And with it paints the sky that changes.

His tomb? What this stern gaze sees
Unravelling, deep in the *Self-Portrait*
Whose silvering, that loved his dream, dulls—

An old man, at evening, astonished,
But still determined to say the colour,
Late, his hand become a mortal thing.

Ulysses Sails Past Ithaca

What is this heap of rock and sand? Ithaca—
Remember, with the bees and olive tree,
The faithful wife and the old dog.
But look, water shines black under your prow.

Stop staring at that shore! It is nothing
But your poor kingdom. You don't mean
To reach out to the man that you are,
You who are done with grief and hope.

Pass, disappoint. Let it slide by. See
How it troughs for you, this other strait,
Memory, haunt of those who would die.

Go! Head now for that other low shore.
Where, in the froth and foam of the surf,
The child you used to be is still at play.

San Biagio, at Montepulciano

Columns, arches, vaults—well he knew
What promises you would not keep,
And that your body like your soul
Shrugs off the hands that want to take.

Space! A lure! Assembling and dismantling clouds,
Quick to demolish hope,
The sky's architects offer more
Than ours, who build on dreams.

He dreamt, oh, he dreamt; but on the appointed day
He put beauty to better use
Understanding that form is in order to die.

And this, his final work—a coin
Whose faces are bare. Of this room
He made both arrow and bow, in the stone.

A God

Here lies a god who understood
No more than us. Who never loved
Like a little child. Who was gauche,
Violent, for lack of clarifying words.

And who died without having fulfilled
His promise, just like us.
Who was constantly surprised at being
What we make of him, in our final days.

He was a son? True, but in revolt,
Who insulted his father, and decided
To die, out of disordered pride.

Who'd have liked, for just one hour, to live
Hand in hand with the child he couldn't be,
Though with so often the very same tears.

A Poet

Did he want to be a torch
And toss it in the sea?
He went far in the puddles
Between over there and the sky.

Then he turned back to us,
But the wind had unwritten him
Though his hand still clutched
At the worlds of the smoke.

Sibyls' scattered sheets,
Torn utterance extreme,
What's he talking about? We never knew.

He believed in simpler words,
But over there is only still here.
And the water's sheen is no sign.

A Stone

He wanted the stone
That would be engraved in his memory
To be one of those clayey slabs
He kicked, down in the ravine.

Their nicks, their mosses, crimson red,
The chaos that makes each one
Indecipherably unique, although the same
As all the rest—there is his epitaph.

He dreamt, he died. Where is his grave?
Hiker, if you scramble down these scarps
Will you notice the words he thought he brought

To the frost-cracked stone? Hear his voice
Under the insect drone? Will you
Casually kick his life even further down?

Tomb of Paul Verlaine

This 'shallow stream'—where does it flow
More sweetly than in his lines, that know
Land is not far, in the tangled
Marshes of desire and dreams?

Judges, when evening comes, the words!
Mud as much as light, truth!
He never forgot this, even when his subjects—
Tiresome, futile—skipped from stone to stone.

Humble, out of simple pride, he agreed
To be for others a mirror only
Whose tarnished silver would filter the sky.

Let them see that the sky in him
Shone reddest through the evening leaves
When the cooing of the wood pigeons dims.

One of Wordsworth's Childhood Memories

As in *The Prelude,* this child who sets out
In the unconscious of the light
And spies a boat and, between earth and sky,
Jumps aboard to row towards another shore;

Then sees, towering up over there, threatening,
A summit, black and huge, behind others,
And is afraid, and turns back to the reeds
Where minimal lives murmur the eternal;

So this great poet will have launched his thoughts
On a calm hour of the language;
He believed himself redeemed by his speech.

But currents, silent, bore his words
Beyond him in their consciousness;
He was afraid to be more than his desire.

REMARKS ON THE HORIZON

Shall we talk about the horizon, my friends; what else is there to talk about?

We are always talking about it, within it rather. When we make plans, when we love.

When we love, for to love—a person, a road, a work of art— is to see that the line over there, so far ahead of us, the line that is all light is here too, passing through them and passing through them again, just as the sea comes and goes on the sand, lifting and dropping the swaying algae, the obscure life.

The line of over-there and the line of here, each tossing the froth of the unconscious under our feet—sentence aglitter from riding this wave, which swells like a night then collapses, then swells again.

I take this road, it is narrow, it plunges between two small buttes, trees cover it, close round me, over me; I'm glad to be familiar with it, with the thousands of lives down in the bottom of it, used to me. Underneath, though, down below the peeping, the rustling, the flying off, that faint but steady sound I hear is the 'over-there' of the skyline which, though unseen, goes with me. Holding the present moment, the moment of being here in its hands, hands that I glimpse, blue or red ochre, through a break in the pines and the scrub oak.

With the sky above me, reminding me that the sky is over there too, and can see below the line where, for us here, what is is out of sight.

And colour, among us, like this secret, which is its secret.

And the cry of that bird which repeats, which is a call. It must come from the other world, bringing back the gold, a bit of straw to line the nest's unseen bottom.

Horizon light also, that water taking its time evaporating, God knows why, from the puddles underfoot.

God? I mean the rain that chose to fall here. Which could have fallen further on in that small wood—hence chance, hence divine.

The horizon thinker has no god—these distances suffice, sliding like water from the bottom of the sky over the marks the child makes in the sand.

The water rises suddenly, the wave erases the signs; afternoon is over, the child climbs back up from the roar of the sea, back among the voices and big naked bodies.

Skyline like the stone I lift from the mud, hollows filled with the smell of salt.

Skyline in the word I see shining under the others, when the unconscious at high tide comes with its clear water to wash the sentences I have set down right on its edge, just to see. Weeds lifted, that fall back, my words undone, but with at their surface for an instant the salt mist of a water that is perhaps the sky.

Words offer their full sense only if we contemplate what they say 'over there', on the line of a horizon. Here we are too close to the details; thought catches in too many aspects, deploys itself in too many formulas—the desire to possess, to understand supplants everything. Over there the whole is more important than the parts, things become beings again.

As when Proust sees 'the Martinville steeples' against the sky. And his whole life to come is affected. Remembering those beings on the horizon, he will look at other beings who are only here; looking for the gold, their presence in the distance, in the vast new crucible.

The blue of distances in words as well, like the dreamt-of meaning in the thing said.

I believe I owe almost everything to the horizons of my early years. Horizons far off, horizons up close, whether open, under big clouds, or withdrawn into the dark water of the river's bend.

And with my biggest debt—'debt' because I know it will be necessary to restitute to the world of the last day what water and fire, sky and earth have given us—owed towards a place so close to me that, had I been someone else, I could have decided that this place was the here, the here in itself. It was the top of a long low hill barely an hour's walk away, where one particular big tree, backlit against the sky, was far enough to signify the absolute but close enough to seem to be a point in this world. To arrive at the foot of it in the late afternoon heat and still have time to discover from under its wide branches the valley, unknown before this instant, and the familiar house!

It is so easy to let oneself dream badly when the horizon is too far! Or when it is right down under the bushes of a vast plain; or worse, when at a distance it gets entangled with low hills where shadows and sun play, with here or there a brightly coloured field. If other than ours are its glitter, its pools, its unfathomable remnants of night in what seem its faults! One can imagine it is not a line but a land, part of it on this side—our side—and part on the other side. A place whose things, whose inhabitants, that you see in your binoculars, are clearly going about their lives, neither here nor there, neither of the known world, nor of the unknown worlds. Who are those people? Our roads no longer take us there. And their roads don't go very far either, on the other side, where what we'd most likely find as we went that way is our very own land again, having passed without seeing it through the space in which the other land lies.

The country on the horizon! The caravans wending their way between our earth and another. The flights into Egypt in our binoculars, vanishing behind a stretch of dune, reappearing farther on. The desperate inadequacy of the binoculars. Scarcely specks of light those faces over there. You might think they aren't faces at all, so many rays of light shine from them, reflecting off others! Maybe gold masks. Maybe eyes so enlarged that they efface the design that, even over there, reduces those here to what we are.

A definition of language—a here that breathes the elsewhere, a medusa as big as a sea which would be the world.

Writing poetry? Earth under our feet but storm-soaked, rutted by big wheels that have driven past, driven on. Earth all ruts whose brief gleams rise.

I come to the puddle, I stop, I look up from the road, I hear the baa-ing of a lamb in the distance, under the now motionless clouds.

A gate creaks—nearly the glitter of the rose in itself. Of the forbidden garden, guarded by a parrot with lightless eyes.

In Melville's tale, the traveller, we are told, has set off from Pittsfield for Mount Greylock, fascinated by a window that at certain hours blazes on his daily horizon. Happy the people who live there, he thinks. He arrives at the house, he opens the gate; enters a room, sees a girl at her window gazing towards his house off in the distance in his other world. Why does he go away again? Out of sympathy, out of love. Doesn't he give a great gift, perhaps the supreme gift? What he offers is not to extinguish the tiny hope on her illusory hearth, understanding that it is the sole good at the moment he renounces it.

So painters humanize landscapes whose lifelong hold on us we may not immediately grasp.

And when all at once the over-there goes missing because here, without warning, is the snow, snow falling with wind to ruffle its light: now at last the horizon is with us, we touch it, we cross it, we cross it again, gropingly, we drink its cold air, this is the blissfulness of snow.

'Horizon'—a word I don't care for; I'd like another one. One that would stretch out a hand from its steep sides to our words, to help them climb towards it into the unseen. A word that would favour the landscape painters among us, assuring them a future Earth needs and yearns for, a cup that has rolled alongside, whose shattering she may one day die from.

ON LEAVING THE GARDEN
A VARIATION

Something imagined, insistent. A man and a woman set out under trees that grow very close together in places, their branches knit even close to the ground, so that several times these two very handsome, very young beings have hesitated to walk on in the frail, pungent crunching of leaves. They've looked round, they seem to have chosen another direction; but also it's early still, the day is young and already the trees thin out, the branches start higher, the edge of the wood is near, soon crossed. Ahead of us now are regions of gentle, greenish-golden hills in which one can readily imagine small lakes hiding, their calm water devoid of boats. It looks deserted, this big country with its beautiful, expansive light.

On they go, the two of them, through more small woods; occasionally they even halt, turning towards each other and, seen from afar, standing as they do, between the last tree and the wide open sky, it's as if they were speaking, the young woman pointing who knows where, to the horizons. Off they go again, but are they not still here, stock still, one might think? All this sky and these trees, and water sensed in the distance might be a painting, one of those predominantly dark green canvases that a painter of 1660 or thereabouts, a descendant of Poussin, one of Gaspar Dughet's friends, might have substituted for the world if from the depths of those mysterious years certain winds had sprung up, as indeed they should have, to sweep from under our feet the long winter's leftover leaves.

A painting. In the form of the shoulders, the arms, in these lines that stand out as when a painter is at work and the colour of the hair or the lovely exposed flesh is almost too bright, and also the foliage, and glimpses of fruit: yes, a painting, for I do know who this man and woman, walking past us on this otherwise deserted earth, are for me. They are Eve and Adam after what has been called the Fall. They have been banished from the Garden of Eden, they cross it unhurriedly, for time hasn't started yet. Nothing but the hours of the summer sky in this land without roads, where light alone decides, laughingly separating the colours that play too ardently, bending to pick one up, that has fallen, that is astonished.

Adam, Eve? They've a whole day to wander the earth, after which, late afternoon, when the sun goes down, the gates will loom up at the end of a long, very long, sandy lane and the wind will have risen, in the west the sky will be red, and in the trees a new kind of bird will be calling. Night waits beyond the threshold's stringent opening, the two outcasts will consent, off they will go into the shadows, but for now they know only this instant, the timeless present of images. Did a voice rend the sky some time before this peaceful morning? Words in what was only rustling water and leaves, did a purple fabric flash through these half-tints? They don't remember, they don't think about it.

They go, is all. Sometimes I lose sight of them, but not because the road they've taken hides them. Simply, I've had other things to think about, elsewhere, three or four times already.

I should say that everywhere silence reigns. The distant squawk of a magpie, some mooing in the fields, the clatter of a stone falling off a cliff and tumbling into the ravine, none of this disturbs the peace; on the contrary, these sounds from the visible world deepen, enlarge and clarify it—as does the heat, increasing, but not without a touch of breeze. I like this silence but I must say it now troubles me as much as once it reassured me. As if a certain sound I heard differed in kind, say, from this stream beside us that never stops lapping at its banks.

A sound. That seems to come from farther away but also nearer than all these intermittent, inconsequential sounds. And what's more, whose startling brevity I couldn't comprehend. Was it just something musical, the echo of a little flute on the plains of another earth, was it a human voice? I listen. And those two beings have reappeared; I see them, yes, they are talking, but quickly decide, it seems to me, to forget what they too heard. Surprised, still dithering perhaps, off they go again in this high noon—already—in which the morning shadows, that were transparent, are going to turn into evening ones.

The afternoon hours, always the day's slowest, most troubling too, since the horizon closes in, colours change. I look at these two beings whom I imagine, I take the same road, I think of eternity and time, of the beauty of bodies, of gestures and who knows what else?

Now, ahead of them, a bush quivers. Branches moved, as if someone had hidden there to see them and had only at the last second fled. Someone? Yes, animals don't run off like that; they stay in their here and now, just as the branch we've pushed aside snaps back into place. Someone who is going to run, into the elsewhere, flop in the grass, leap up, run again, then stop, seem to think it over, come back. Someone? Fairly light and very nimble, lithe. Is that the voice that called from the other side of the visible, the little dreaming flute? Yes, it is indeed a child on the prowl, naked, unselfconscious, in all this solitude.

And who does indeed steal back. During this day that a moment spreads out before us then dims I know I'm going to meet him again, three or four times on the path of the man and woman, eager to see them, wanting to be seen by them and at the same time afraid. He lets them get ahead, he catches up, maybe even in the end, they'll glimpse his large wild eyes staring at them—before the leaves again shut out this perhaps unsettled gaze.

It's so hard to talk to each other! Silence? It's water, a surface to dip an arm into for what glints on sandy white shadow-crossed bottom; and will we ever reach the thing we hope to grasp? I fear not, a mysterious diffraction plays with us, irresistibly deflecting our hand to one side of our desire's object.—On they go, side by side, the afternoon also turns into brilliance and shadows, I see them lean a moment against a rock, they are talking. Are they alone? There is movement in this stillness, the evening sky's clear fabric shivers as the wind comes up.

I think of the last time, after how many others, how to know, when this child found himself near them, spying on them, about to throw himself at their feet but holding back, why? Did he understand that it was right there, right away, that everything was going to come to an end, and because of this did he desire even more, and then renounce with all the more chagrin or dark joy, after which he recommenced wandering in the eternal? Was it before or after this day that he picked up the reed, touched the sound, invented the sound, introduced some pain and some hope into life? I also wonder why painting preoccupies me, or the image in painting—the water where what is seems to offer itself for a second time but now merely as a reflection, without much quivering in the form that the games of light and shadow dilute.

ANOTHER VARIATION

They fled; damnation's sheet plastered them with rain and lightning. Under their bare feet earth turned to sharp stones, treacherous roots, muck. Their legs stuck in holes they had to jerk them out of. The boy was holding the girl by the hand; something in this contact already filled him, and her too, with more than astonishment. Then the cry: she has fallen, blood trickles down her left leg, a red new in the world, and he—he helps her up but her ankle buckles; Eve must lean on Adam's arm to limp towards the unknown ahead of them in the unknown that surrounds them, under the black sky's unknown. Night now, and how to walk when each step adds to the pain? Steps that grow harder and harder as the outer chaos spreads to another, within these two, who walk on without knowing or wanting anything except to be elsewhere, far. Steps? Blundering, rather, into thick limbs in the dark, water all of a sudden drenching the arms that grope through the leaves. Not so much wanting to get through these endless thickets as to stop—stop the wind, the rain, forget the voice in the sky that keeps harassing them. Yes, forget? The need too, now overwhelming, to sink onto the bed of grass whose vague phosphorescence, all soft and wavy, has begun to look almost welcoming, what a surprise, between the trunks of trees that make room.

They drop down, first a knee, the flat of the hand, fast the whole body, onto the drenched grass, but the rain is warm, like a gift they've been given, and now here they are lying side by side, very close, what is time begins, between them a gaze, compassion, desire. He touches the hurt leg; he fears, on this face, so near, pain's grimace; in fact, he is discovering it—the face—had he seen it before? Eyes in which astonishment grows and fades. Lips. Adam and Eve see one another, recognize each other, know each other, as will be said; it doesn't take long, a different haste, also a sharing, all the same, that ties them to each other towards they don't know what, in another sort of night.

And again, farther away now, it seems, the sky sounds as before with lightning still, maybe less frequently, and in the bushes about the man and the woman, watchful, other, quieter noises, fluttering wings, minimal unseen lives that don't disturb them, that envelop them rather, another sheet, for this becomes sleep, which is new on earth too. Perception's porosity: between inner and outer now nothing is still, forms unravel, others are born in them, what is, what is not?

Agitation of the first dreams, glimmers too, in the hands that now and then touch, and when they wake everything is different—yesterday's turmoil is gone; here or there light gleams through clouds still grey or black. Eve is feeling better, thank goodness; she can stand, hobble forward, under the uncertain vault—yes, but first how about giving some thought to this life that has sprung up in night's intimacy, this other life, the life of words, of speech, whispered and as if feverish?

It is Eve who speaks up, in a burst of enthusiasm with, I think, a little fear, why?

'Listen,' she says quietly, bent over the face lit by sunbeams strewn by the big clouds' prism. 'Listen, yesterday, you didn't finish the naming.'

Him: 'True. I'd given a name to the stream. Then I saw how it widened over there where sand mixed with the stones and reeds. The water ran less quickly. A strange bird landed, kept perfectly quiet, then flapped its wings, flew off, came back, why, flew off again, and came back again. I heard something rustle on the shore, I smelt things, savoury, mint, it doesn't matter, together all these things existed more than each thing for itself—the sand, the bird, the rustling under leaves. I wanted to give a name, a single simple big name, to this moment, no, not a moment, to all this—what's the word?—to this peace. Give a name also to that space I saw slowly changing—blue, no, not blue exactly, pink just as much, a golden pink—between two clouds. Or again to the marks traced for nothing on sand when the water falls back.

'Then I heard the shot, I don't know where from, and I saw the bird slump, drag itself to the sand and flap its wings. Sand spurted up, dropped over it, covered it, it twitched a little, it stopped moving. I stopped feeling like naming things.'

Eve looks at her fingers, she fans them out and in like a game. 'Me,' she says, 'I'd like to give a name to just that, simply, the black, the black in eyes, the black when that's all there is, when nothing else remains.'

They've stood up. Along Eve's mud-splattered leg the blood has dried. Cautiously she picks the brown earth off. In the distance thunder still rumbles, nothing really black, swirls of colour such as painters will make. And huge, sudden drenching rains, then the sky comes back above what words will have to make a sort of earth of.